The Four Keys to Advertising Success

The Four Keys to Advertising Success

A 1-Hour Guide for Small Business Owners

Spike Santee

Copyright © 2011 by Spike Santee.

| ISBN: | Softcover | 978-1-4628-6503-1 |
| | Ebook | 978-1-4628-6504-8 |

All rights reserved. No part of this book may be reproduced or transmitted in any form or by any means, electronic or mechanical, including photocopying, recording, or by any information storage and retrieval system, without permission in writing from the copyright owner.

This book was printed in the United States of America.

To order additional copies of this book, contact:
Xlibris Corporation
1-888-795-4274
www.Xlibris.com
Orders@Xlibris.com
98727

Contents

1. Why Write a Book About Local Advertising?...................11
2. The Four Keys to Advertising Success: An Overview 15
3. Have a Written Business Plan 21
4. Is Your Business Plan on Track? 27
5. How to Survey Your Customers........................31
6. Consistency—The First Key to Advertising Success......................35
7. Reach—The Second Key to Advertising Success..........................39
8. Frequency—The Third Key to Advertising Success 43
9. Compelling Creative Message—The Fourth Key.......................49
10. The Psychology of Consumer Behavior 53
11. Advertising Creates Awareness......................61
12. The Decision Journey..............................65
13. Parting Thoughts: The Law of Seed Time to Harvest 77

This book is dedicated to my family. First, I dedicate this book to my grandfather and mother, whose hard work in tough times made it possible for me to enjoy the life I live today. They taught me the value and benefit of having a strong work ethic. Second, I dedicate this book to my wife Trena and my two sons Weston and Hollis. They are my inspiration to be a better person. They are my motivation to live up to the work ethic taught to me by my mother and grandfather.

I want to thank my editor Sharon Boranyak at *www.sharonwritesforyou.com*. Sharon helped me pull all of my writings together, get organized and complete the project. She immersed herself in this project and viewed the material through her paradigm of a small business owner.

Even though they have passed on to that great Radio Ranch in the sky, I'd like to thank Mike Oatman and Mike Lynch for letting me join the Great Empire Broadcasting Ranch Hands. It was at the Radio Ranch in Wichita Kansas where I learned the valuable lessons about how Radio advertising really can work for the local business owner. The "Mikes" taught me important life lessons too, especially how to treat your customers and your fellow coworkers with respect and dignity. Everybody has a story.

Finally, I would like to thank all of the business owners who have allowed me to work with them over the years to help them grow and prosper in their business efforts. It is those experiences that form the basis of my book.

"You can have everything in life you want, if you will just help enough other people get what they want."—Zig Ziglar, author and motivational speaker (1926-

1

Why Write a Book About Local Advertising?

I started selling advertising in 1972, working for the high school newspaper in Lawrence, Kansas. We didn't earn a commission for selling the ads in the newspaper; selling the ads was a part of our grade for the class.

Since those days as a high school kid selling display ads in the high school newspaper, I've had the privilege of working with thousands of business owners across the country. They live the American dream of building a life and making a living in the free enterprise system. They are inspirational because they risk everything to be the backbone of American business.

Local business owners learn about advertising and marketing the hard way, at the School of Hard Knocks. They have experimented with their hard earned-money, trying this, testing that, as they build their advertising and marketing knowledge base. For many, this knowledge base is filled with failed advertising and market experiments that have wasted thousands of dollars. It's not really the business owner's fault. There are legions of unscrupulous advertising sales people out there hawking their latest *advertising package* promising all kinds of glorious results.

These failed experiments have been so costly and the memories are so painful that many business owners have concluded that advertising doesn't pay. They even go so far as to rationalize that their business is so unique that advertising and marketing doesn't apply for their special situation. Too many business owners, in frustration, simply give up trying to advertise or market their business altogether. Simply pulling in your advertising resources and hoping that consumers will find you by reputation or through a search engine on the Internet simply isn't practical, nor is it a smart business strategy.

Half of Advertising Money Is Wasted

John Wannamaker introduced the first department store to Philadelphia consumers in 1875. His store became so successful that he soon had stores in New York City, London and Paris. Wannamaker was one of America's first big advertisers and is considered by many to be the Father of Modern Advertising.

It was John Wannamaker who once said "Half of the money I spend on advertising is wasted. The problem is I don't know which half."

More than 135 years later, Wannamaker's words resonate with most small business owners. Many entrepreneurs don't know how—or simply don't have time—to measure advertising results. Consequently, they learn about advertising the hard way, spending their hard-earned money on trial and error. They are confused, too, because of all the different claims made by advertising vendors, competing for their business.

If you have experienced similar feelings of frustration and confusion in trying to advertise your business, this book is for you.

The Four Keys to Advertising Success will help you **stop the frustration and confusion and move on** to a new level of understanding.

This is a book about **local advertising**, written for and about the **local small business owner.** The Four Keys are based on my 35 years of experience of helping thousands of local small businesses achieve their goals. To understand how the Four Keys can work for your business, I also review important business planning fundamentals you need to have in place, and consumer behavior fundamentals you need to remember, as you implement the Four Keys.

This book is a practical 1-hour guide on how to make advertising work for your business. It's a series of small chapters to make it easy for you to reference when you're faced with advertising decisions. Happy- and productive-reading!

"We can't solve problems by using the same kind of thinking we used when we created them."—Albert Einstein, scientist (1879-1955)

2

The Four Keys to Advertising Success: An Overview

For the first 20 years of my advertising and marketing career, I met hundreds, if not thousands, of business owners who struggled with this question regarding their advertising: "What works and what doesn't work?" I'd also heard comments about their past advertising experiences: "I tried advertising once, it didn't work." Better yet, "I tried *radio* or I tried *newspaper* or I tried *cable* advertising once and it didn't work." Insert any form of advertising and the refrain was often the same: "I tried it and it didn't work."

This is a common feeling among business owners. They've tried to advertise but they've been disappointed with the results. Many business owners who place an advertising plan and are then disappointed with the results will say that the *advertising didn't work*. The business owner is quick to blame the **medium**. We find out, though, that the medium did its part. We know that consumers were exposed to the advertising message from the circulation figures, traffic counts, viewer and listener estimates. Indeed, consumers were exposed to the message. However, the consumers said "No." Chances are, the real reason for the disappointing response to the advertising may have been the **message** didn't resonate with the consumers; or perhaps the ad didn't **reach** the target audience—two key elements may have been missing.

I found that the root cause of a business owner's disappointment is that they don't have a grasp of how advertising works—how certain key elements need to come together.

The Research

In 1992, I had the perfect opportunity to find the answer to the question: "What works and what doesn't work?" That year, I joined a large broadcasting company with over 1,000 small businesses that advertised with the company each year. With 1,000 businesses to talk to, I could conduct some comparative research between business owners who said their advertising *worked* and business owners who said their advertising *didn't work*. With such a large pool of businesses, I had plenty of both kinds of research subjects.

When the research began, the subject business owners were divided into two groups: satisfied business owners/advertisers, "advertising worked" and dissatisfied business owners/advertisers, "advertising didn't work." The vast majority of business owners in the research had no formal training or education in advertising and marketing. The only criterion for separating the business owners into the two control groups was their own *opinion* about their advertising.

The goal of the research was to identify the key factors of success that the satisfied advertisers used. The research found a common thread of four key elements that were always present in the successful campaigns: a commitment to a **consistent** plan, the proper mix of **reach** and **frequency** for the advertising budget, and an **emotional, engaging message** about the business. Thus emerged *The Four Keys to Advertising Success.*

The campaigns considered successful included **all four** key elements, while those not considered successful were missing one or more of these key variables.

As the research evolved, we started to show the dissatisfied advertisers these four key elements and encouraged them to include them in their advertising plans. Once they agreed to do so, it took about **four to six months** for the formerly dissatisfied advertisers to report that they were **feeling better about their advertising efforts**. They also reported that they began to **understand** how to make advertising work for their business.

Four Keys = Satisfaction

The research, having taken place over several years among thousands of business owners, showed a real correlation between the **presence of the four key factors** in the business owners' advertising and marketing efforts, and the **level of satisfaction** expressed by the business owners. At the same time, the research uncovered even more fascinating information, specifically, the conditions or actions that cause a business owner to become dissatisfied in the first place.

"BADvertising" = Dissatisfaction

My good friend Jason Skaggs first shared with me the word *BADvertising*. I'm borrowing this term from Jason to describe the pitfalls that lead to dissatisfaction among advertisers.

Dissatisfied advertisers—including those who started to implement the Four Keys but later ignored them—succumbed to "The Four Pitfalls of BADvertising":

- The lack of a written business plan and **poor business practices**; no amount of good advertising will overcome bad business decisions.
- Succumbing to the desire for instant gratification; in other words, **becoming impatient** and **inconsistent**.
- Letting your **reach** and **frequency** get **out of balance**; again becoming impatient.
- Trying to advertise your business from the inside out; **not listening to the customer**.

It has become clear to me in hundreds of meetings with business owners/research subjects that you have to fully understand the pitfalls of BADvertising at the same time we learn about *The Four Keys to Advertising Success*. You have to fully understand the negative consequences of BADvertising to realize why you need to stick with *The Four Keys to Advertising Success*. This is why this guide includes chapters to help you identify—and avoid—the pitfalls that will get in the way of your success.

The next three chapters of this guide review the **basic business fundamentals** you need have in place *before* you implement the Four Keys—or even think about purchasing advertising for your business:

- Having a written **business plan**
- **Keeping** your **business** plan **on track**
- **Surveying your customers**, including questions and techniques you can use

Then, I devote four chapters explaining the Four Keys—**consistency, reach, frequency** and **engaging message**.

The remainder of this guide contains equally important **psychological fundamentals** you need to bear in mind as you apply the Four Keys:

- What you need to know about **consumer behavior**, and
- The "journeys" customers take when making their **buying decisions**.

If you find yourself becoming **impatient and tempted ignore the Four Keys, please read and re-read these later chapters!** You'll realize that for advertising to work for your business, you will need to resist the temptation for instant gratification. It takes time for customers to get to know you and to make decisions about your product or service.

As you can see, *The Four Keys to Advertising Success* don't just happen. They are tactics that you employ on a daily basis. Merely implementing *The Four Keys to Advertising Success* is not enough to assure business success. You have to have a goal-driven business plan, constantly make sure your business stays on track, continuously seek feedback from your customers to assure your products and services are relevant and customer-worthy, and—most important—resist the temptation for instant gratification.

"You were not born a winner, and you were not born a loser. You are what you make yourself be."—Lou Holtz, coach, sportscaster, author, and motivational speaker (1937-

3

Have a Written Business Plan

The absence of a goal-driven business plan with a comprehensive marketing strategy to develop a customer base is one of the leading causes of business failure, according to the U.S. Small Business Administration.

Unless your business has the fundamentals in place, even the best advertising in the world won't help. In fact, good advertising can destroy your business. The next few chapters of this book review those fundamentals—planning and goal-setting, and knowing your customers.

In 1979, a study began that involved the students in the Harvard MBA program. In that year, the students were asked, "Have you set clear, written goals for your future and made plans to accomplish them?" Only 3 percent of the graduates had written goals and plans; 13 percent had goals, but they were not in writing; and a whopping 84 percent had no specific goals at all.

Ten years later, the members of the class were interviewed again, and the findings, while somewhat predictable, were nonetheless astonishing. The 13 percent of the class who had goals were earning, on average, twice as much as the 84 percent who had no goals at all.

How did the 3 percent of the graduating class who had clear, written goals perform? They were earning, on average, 10 times as much as the other 97 percent put together.

Setting clear written goals for a business is just the first step. Many local business owners set goals and still struggle. In order to achieve business goals, you must develop a specific written plan. Many local business owners set goals and make written plans to achieve those goals and they still struggle.

Competing Priorities

One of the biggest pitfalls of running a local business is losing sight of your goals. Every morning the local business owner is besieged with issues. Every issue is demanding attention, right now! In a short span of time, that local business owner could find themselves and their business headed in a completely different direction than the original course. But they wouldn't know it because they are dealing with a priority that seems to need their attention at that very moment. They are so busy responding, they don't perceive how far off course they have drifted.

These day-to-day issues are **competing priorities**. Without some discipline, it is easy for the local business owner to become distracted and lose focus on the major goals of their company. If you feel as if there isn't enough time in the day to get everything done, then you are probably a victim of **competing priorities**. The issues you face every day are important. Realize, though, that some issues are more important than others.

To avoid becoming a victim of your competing priorities, **write them down and rank them** in order of importance and deal with them accordingly. Have clear, specific and written goals—a business plan—to keep you from losing your way. Without a written plan, the competing priorities are more likely to take over, and your business will drift off course in a completely different direction than the goals you set. Likewise, if you don't rank your competing priorities, you will become so busy responding to issues that you may drift off course from your goals without even realizing it.

The Passion to Succeed

Developing a business plan and setting clear written goals for a business, though, is just the first step. Many local business owners set goals and make written plans to achieve those goals but they still struggle. The most successful business owners come in to work every day with an undying passion to work on their written plans with everything they have until their business dreams come true.

You have the same amount of time in a day as Oprah Winfrey, Warren Buffett and Bill Gates. You see, it isn't an issue of not having enough time to get everything done. The issue is there isn't enough focus.

Resources to Help You Plan and Focus

You may argue that super-successful business owners like Oprah and Warren have advisers at their disposal to help them stay on track. However, did you know that resources are available to **you**—many of them free of charge—in your own community to help your business succeed?

Organizations such as SCORE (Service Corps of Retired Executives) provides such one-on-one counseling as help with your business plan and goal-setting. Another resource is your local chamber of commerce. Many chambers across the country offer classes and training programs for emerging and existing small businesses. Many universities have small business development centers that offer counseling and services to small businesses. The consultations and classes will point you to the most effective goal-setting and time-management tools and techniques available. The key is to find what works for you and then stick with it day in and day out.

Is Now the Time to Start a Business?

In addition to business owners, I have talked to **prospective** business owners throughout my 35-year career. Many of these prospective business owners are afraid to pursue their dreams when times are tough. The usual excuses include the high rate of unemployment, credit is hard to come by and the news is bad.

Now is just as good as any other time for you to pursue your business dreams. The resources I've just mentioned—SCORE, small business development centers, and entrepreneurial training programs—can help you determine whether your business idea is feasible and give you the confidence to move forward. At the same time, if your business idea is not feasible, these organizations can help you avoid business failure.

You may be surprised, but many successful businesses have started during tough economic times. For example, Leo and Lillian Goodwin lived in Fort Worth, Texas, back in 1936, the worst year of the Great Depression. Unemployment was near 30 percent. Credit was hard to come by. Banks had no money to loan. And the news was bad. War in Europe was on the horizon.

It was that year that Leo decided the time was right for him to start his own insurance company. He had a business idea that had never been tried before. He was going to specialize in car insurance. He felt he could keep his costs down and still make a profit by specializing.

That was a risky proposition in 1936 because the great love affair with the automobile and the open road would come much later, in the 1950s, with the introduction of the Interstate Highway System.

But Leo had another twist to his plans. He was going to specialize in car insurance for government employees. That made some sense because at least the government employees had jobs and money to pay for insurance.

So in 1936, the Goodwins created the Government Employee Insurance Company. They made some goals. They made plans to reach those goals and they worked on those plans every single day and within the first year they had written 3,700 policies and hired a staff of 12 people. Over the years they adapted and expanded as times changed and thrived during several major recessions.

Today, GEICO (Government Employee Insurance Company), built on ingenuity, perseverance, innovation, resilience and hard, honest work, has over 20 million policy holders and has grown to be the third-largest auto insurer in the business. From its humble beginnings in the midst of the Great Depression to its current place as one of the most successful companies in the nation, GEICO represents a quintessential American success story. So today could very well be as good a time as any for you to pursue your business dreams.

There is even more compelling evidence that now is the time to make **goals** for your future. More than half of the businesses that were on the 2009 Fortune 500 list began during a recession or a bear market.

According to the Ewing Marion Kauffman Foundation Index of Entrepreneurial Activity, 558,000 new businesses were created each month in 2009. That means that right now, someone is starting a new business that is one day going to be a future financial powerhouse and it might as well be you. Now is just as good a time as any.

In fact, the Kauffman Foundation sponsors "Fasttrac" entrepreneurial training throughout much of the U.S. Check them out. Go to www.kauffman.org and click on Entrepreneurship; or go to http://fasttrac.org. Now is just as good a time as any.

"The road to success is dotted with many tempting parking places."—Author Unknown

4

Is Your Business Plan on Track?

Staying focused on your business plan to achieve your business goals is an ongoing process. Before you spend another dollar on advertising your business, you should examine whether or not your business is on the right track. Is your business competitive within the market? Do you have the selection, pricing and service that put you at the top of your category? Do your customers enjoy a quality experience when doing business with you? If not, your advertising may be killing your business.

Good Advertising Can Kill Your Business

Consider the following statement: "No amount of good advertising will fix a bad restaurant!" Indeed, no amount of good advertising will fix a bad restaurant or any other business for that matter.

If the restaurant owner isn't willing to address the issues that make his restaurant a poor dining experience, the good advertising will simply let more people know about his restaurant. Those new patrons will have a bad experience and they will tell even more people how bad it is. The increase in bad customer experiences will simply contribute to the negative **brand** consumers have of the restaurant.

In fact, the good advertising may actually accelerate the demise of the bad restaurant because many more people will know firsthand just how bad the dining experience at that restaurant can be.

Your business brand isn't merely your logo or your slogan. Your business **brand is the mental image the consumer has when they hear or see**

your business name. Your business brand is what people say about you to their friends.

Simply put, no amount of good advertising can overcome the bad business practices of the owner. If the business isn't ready for the new customers, that will lead to a poor experience. If the business doesn't have the right products at the right prices, that will lead to a disappointing customer experience. If the business can't support the sales process, if they can't deliver on the promises made during the sale, then the customer will leave with a very poor image of the business.

The owner of the bad restaurant can advertise all day every day but advertising won't improve the quality of the food, won't improve the speed or friendliness of the service and can't make the prices competitive with other similar restaurants.

I doubt that the bad restaurant owner wants to have a bad restaurant. In all probability, he is unaware just how bad the dining experience at his restaurant has become. That's because many business owners are so busy trying to run their business, they don't have time to step back and see their business from the consumer's point of view.

Step Back, Evaluate

It's not hard to understand why a small business owner can fall into this trap of only seeing their business from the inside out. Many small business owners lack formal business training. They got into business because they were good at their trade or they grew up in the business. For many it seems only natural that they should start a business because they're good at what they do. But being good at what you do is only part of the formula for business success.

Another reason a business owner can fall into the trap of only seeing their business from their own perspective is pride. For many business owners, running a business is not a 9 to 5 job. They often spend 12, 16 maybe even 18 hours a day, every day working to build their business. It's all they think about. They pour their heart and soul into the business. They put everything they have into the business. They may even have their name on the business. They take a lot of pride in their business.

But that pride may be the very thing that prevents the business owner from honestly evaluating their position within the market place. That pride may drive the business owner to discredit any legitimate or constructive criticism of the business. They may dismiss the criticism because they don't feel the person knows what they are talking about. "They don't spend 18 hours a day working here like I do," the owner may think.

All that the advertising can do is to inform the public about the business. Advertising will let people know what the business is, where the business is located and what that business does. The minute the new customer walks into the front door of the business, the rest is up to the business owner. No amount of advertising can change what happens when the customer arrives at the business. It is now up the business owner to follow through.

Get the Customer's Point of View

If the business owner cannot objectively evaluate and improve on the customer experience from the customer's point of view, the business will surely fail no matter how much advertising they buy.

Gaining objectivity about your business can be a very difficult endeavor because you will learn things about your business that will hurt your feelings. In the next chapter, I share some survey methods that will help you learn things about your business that fly in the face of everything you've ever thought about your business. You will learn things about your business that will be hard to believe. You may even learn that you should just sell the business and go get a job working for someone else.

"What you see depends on what you're looking for."
—Anonymous

5

How to Survey Your Customers

It's absolutely essential that your future business decisions are based on the customer's point of view and not your own. I present some proven techniques in the next few paragraphs, but I strongly suggest that you get someone to help you with this. Otherwise, if you do this on your own you will filter everything through your own viewpoint.

You don't necessarily have to hire an outside consultant to conduct the survey. Chances are, the business school at the local college is looking for a marketing research project. Many high schools, too, have entrepreneurial programs and would welcome a project like yours. If nothing else is available, have one of your employees conduct the survey.

The Customer's Point of View

If you must do the survey on your own with your own employee asking the questions, keep the survey questions simple and to a minimum. Here are some examples:

1. Is this your first visit to our company?
2. What other companies did you consider before coming to us?
3. Why did you choose our store?
    a. Price
    b. Selection
    c. Location
    d. Reputation
    e. Previous experience

4. How would you rate your customer experience?
   a. Very satisfied
   b. Satisfied
   c. Dissatisfied
   d. Very dissatisfied
5. What would you say to your friends about shopping with us?
6. Would you like to receive emails about upcoming specials and events?

In addition:

- Print your survey on some nice paper.
- Make sure there is a place for the customer to write their name, address, phone number and email.
- Have a disclaimer on the survey that it is a private survey for internal use only and you won't be sharing their information with anyone else.
- Consider giving the survey participant a coupon for their next visit as a "thank you" for taking time to answer your questions.

Don't succumb to the desire to ask the customer "How did you hear about us?" You won't get any legitimate responses. People don't really know how they learned about your business. You can't draw a conclusive connection between your advertising and why the customer is on your doorstep. We know this because customers will give us **false positives** when they respond. You'll inevitably get someone to say they saw your commercial on TV and that's what brought them in. It is a **false positive** because you've never ever advertised on TV.

Media Usage Surveys

If you do want to survey media usage, then do it this way.

1. Do you have a paid subscription to the local newspaper?
2. What is your favorite radio station?
3. What TV station do you turn to for local news and weather?
4. Do you subscribe to cable TV?
5. Do you subscribe to satellite TV? If so, which service?

From this information you may be able to see some patterns or trends. If you see that a particular TV station or radio station is showing up in your research and you don't advertise there, then perhaps you should. There is something compatible with the audience of that medium and your business. There is some socioeconomic connection between that medium and your business that you can tap into.

You should start to see media that you *do* advertise on eventually show up in your survey. But keep in mind this takes time. Students of the psychology of consumer behavior and the physiology of the human brain know that the buying cycle is much longer than you know or wish it to be.

Once you begin the process of surveying your customers, you must keep doing it over the long term to see any trends. You must try to survey all of your customers in order to get a clear picture of how they feel.

When the comments come in, read every single one and take to heart what they say—even if the comments are painful. Your customers are the people who do business with your company and who put money in your pocket. Don't lose sight of that. You are in business to provide products and services for your customers. It's all about them. It's not about you.

"Continuous effort, not strength or intelligence, is the key to unlocking our potential."—Winston Churchill, British Prime Minister (1874-1965)

6

Consistency—The First Key to Advertising Success

The First Key to Advertising Success is consistency. It is also the most difficult of the Four Keys to practice because we live in a world of *instant gratification*. We have grown accustomed to getting what we want when we want it. In today's high-speed, on-line world, a consumer can go on to the Internet and order what they want and have it delivered within hours. We hate to wait. Just like everything else, it's natural to want instant results from your advertising efforts.

Making a commitment to a consistent plan is the fundamental building block of success in everything, including advertising your business. But don't confuse consistency with spending a lot of money. Consistency is not about how much money you spend on advertising every year. Consistency is all about establishing an amount of money you can spend consistently on advertising, year after year after year.

Consumer perception studies often show the company with the higher awareness scores in the market is not the company that spends the most money but the company that has been **consistently** advertising the longest.

The Temptation of Instant Gratification

The biggest mistake you can make in advertising is to expect instant gratification from your advertising efforts. It is a natural urge to want instant results but to do so ignores the natural order of things that occur in the consumer's life. Successful advertising depends on gaining an understanding of what your prospects go through before they make a decision to do business with you. "The Decision Journey" later in this guide explains this in more detail.

We have all heard the idiom "Haste makes waste," acting too quickly (haste), and making mistakes, and then ending up with poor results (waste). "Haste makes waste" teaches us that it is better to do things carefully than to do them quickly and carelessly. This is exceptionally true when it comes to your advertising.

In pursuit of instant gratification from an advertising investment, a business owner or manager will often **hastily** move their advertising from one medium to the next when they don't feel as if they are getting the results they want as quickly as they want. If that business owner or manager understood the natural laws that govern consumer behavior, they would realize that about the time they hastily move their advertising to a new medium, the consumers using the previous medium were just starting to become aware of the business. In other words, the awareness of that business with the consumers was finally reaching the level where consumers would start to respond. But the advertising drops from view and the business loses that little foot hold in the consumer's mind called awareness.

No matter what kind of advertising you decide to do, make the commitment to stick with it for the long haul. Business goes where business is invited. Your advertising is your invitation. When you're not advertising, you're not inviting. The most satisfied advertisers keep inviting their customers.

Consistency is the hallmark of virtually every advertising campaign that was considered to be effective by the business owners themselves. Whether they set out to be consistent or not is hard to determine. What *is* clear is the long-term consistent advertiser was more satisfied with their efforts than the business owner who followed a less-consistent strategy.

Consistency Takes Long-Term Commitment

Advertising is a lot like exercise. If you are out of shape and overweight, we all know that going to the gym one time isn't going to fix the problem. You will need to make a commitment to go to the gym on a regular basis a few times a week to make a difference.

Setting an advertising budget is similar to weight lifting. Start out with a budget that is challenging but something you can maintain. Add more advertising as your business strength improves. Don't start out with such a big advertising commitment that you "pull a financial muscle" and injure your business. You'll have to sit out until you recuperate, or even worse, quit advertising altogether.

As you learn more about consumer psychology and human behavior, you will see why consistency is the First Key to Advertising Success. Your advertising efforts must be well trained and in top shape in order to perform when the consumers find themselves in need of what you have to offer.

The buying process is more about human behavior and the thought process consumers go through than about you and your advertising because advertising doesn't cause people to buy things. Advertising doesn't make people come into your store. Advertising doesn't make people pick up the phone to call you or to go on-line to your web site. These are the intended consequences of your advertising efforts. It is essential to your success that you understand this basic premise: **People buy when they have a need or a desire for a product or a service.**

"The consumer isn't a moron. She is your wife." David Ogilvy, advertising pioneer and founder of Ogilvy Advertising (1911-1999)

7

Reach—The Second Key to Advertising Success

Reach is the term used to describe how many people will see or hear an advertisement. Many business owners are already familiar with the term reach. We know this because one of the first questions a business owner will ask the advertising salesperson is "How many people will drive by my billboard?" or "How many homes will get my direct mail piece?" or "How many people will hear my commercial?"

When analyzing reach, it is important not to confuse the medium's audience size with the reach of the small business owner's advertising message. Many media sales people lead their presentation with a description of their subscriber base or viewing or listening audience. The **size of the medium's audience is *not* the reach of your advertising message**.

The newspaper salesperson may say the newspaper has 100,000 subscribers. That is the **circulation** of the newspaper, not the **reach** of a display ad in the paper. For example, if the display ad is in the sports section of the newspaper, only those readers who read the sports section have a chance of seeing that display advertisement. If the advertisement is small in size, there is a chance that not all of the sports section readers will see it. Depending on many factors, there is a very good chance that the reach of the display advertisement could be much smaller than the newspaper's total circulation.

If you want to reach to total circulation of the newspaper, you would have to buy many display ads in all of the sections of the newspaper over all of the days of the week. Even then, you wouldn't reach all of the newspaper's paid circulation. Some of their subscribers might be on vacation that week and not read the newspaper at all.

The TV salesperson may claim that the TV station has 100,000 viewers. That is the **viewership** of the television station, not the **reach** of your TV commercial. Maybe the salesperson narrows down the audience estimate to just the viewers of the 6:00 news. One commercial in that 30-minute time slot won't reach all of the viewers. Maybe some of them tune in late. Perhaps others want to watch only the weather. Some tune in only for the top stories.

In order to reach all of the viewers of the 6:00 news, you would need to buy several commercials within the newscast.

Now with new technology like DVR, experts estimate that when viewers are watching on a delayed basis, anywhere from 50 to 70 percent of the commercials are passed over so the viewer can skip ahead to the next scene in the show.

The radio station salesperson may claim that the radio station has 100,000 listeners. That is the **listenership** of the radio station, not the **reach** of your radio campaign. If you run your radio commercials only in "drive time," the listeners who work overnight won't hear your commercial.

Every medium has the ability to tell the small business owner what their reach will be. All you need to do is ask. Make sure you ask, "**How many people will see/hear my advertisement?**"

"Repetition makes reputation and reputation makes customers."
Elizabeth Arden, founder of Elizabeth Arden Cosmetics (1884-1966)

8

Frequency—The Third Key to Advertising Success

Reach has a cousin, frequency, the Third Key to Advertising Success. The most satisfied advertisers in our research study were those small business owners who had achieved a natural balance between both reach and frequency. That balance is dictated by the advertising budget you establish.

The dissatisfied advertisers often had an imbalance between reach and frequency. The two most common causes of this imbalance were the small business owner's ego and the advertising salesperson's media hype. The two are often partners that steer the small business owner in the wrong direction.

Since advertising the small business owner's business is often a direct reflection on the small business owner themselves, their ego can get easily involved in their advertising. A crafty commission-driven media salesperson will often exploit the small business owner's ego to make an "easy" sale. The salesperson will talk all about "their" product, building it up in importance while never really addressing the real issue of the balance between reach and frequency.

In other words, when ego and salesmanship drive the decision-making process, the balance between reach and frequency is often the casualty because the small business owner has been seduced by the "sizzle" of the advertising salesperson's sales pitch.

It's Not About You

For example, many small business owners want to advertise in the media that they themselves consume. If they watch the number one TV news show, they often want to advertise in the show they watch. They watch that show; they perceive that all of their friends watch that show, so that's where they feel they need to advertise. Their ego wants to advertise in that TV show because they are focused solely on the reach. They will tell their friends, "Yep, I'm advertising on WXYZ TV, the biggest TV station in town."

But if their ego exceeds their advertising budget, they may not be able to buy enough commercials to achieve enough **frequency**. So they have the potential to reach a lot of people with their message but they don't have enough budget to buy **enough** commercials to achieve a level of effective frequency. Lots of people may see the small business owner's television ad, but most people won't see it enough times, **frequently enough**, for the message to **sink in and be effective**. Many people simply won't see the small business owner's commercial at all.

The challenges of trying to achieve a balance between reach and frequency is only exacerbated by the inherent imbalance many media have based on their pricing structure. Advertising on a medium with a large audience is naturally going to cost more than a similar medium with a smaller audience.

The Balancing Act

Reaching the largest audience sounds reasonable to many small business owners. But without adequate frequency, that advertising budget will be wasted. If the small business owner can take their ego out of the mix and consider advertising on a **medium with a smaller audience where they can get more commercials** and consequently more frequency, they have a much better balance between reach and frequency. This can be a challenge because the small business owner must come to grips with the limitations of their advertising budget. They may have to face the reality that they cannot afford to be on the "big" station.

Don't Forget Consistency!

For the majority of small business owners, branding or image advertising is the first order of business. If done correctly, branding/image advertising can be very effective and affordable. But the small business owner must follow the First Key to Advertising Success: ***consistency***.

Consistency isn't about how much money the small business owner spends. Consistency is about how long they spend the money they have budgeted on the same medium. The overwhelming body of evidence indicates that to be effective, an **advertisement must reach the consumer a minimum of three different times within seven days** from the first exposure to the advertisement.

Beware of media sales people who use the term "average frequency of three." "Average frequency of three" means some consumers will be exposed to your message only once, some will be exposed to your message more than that. You want to know how many people will **hear** your message three or more times. That is your **effective reach**.

Spread Too Thin

But if a small business owner is trying to have a special sale or a big promotion they will need to do "Call to Action" advertising. Call to Action advertising is very expensive. It requires a lot more money in a very short period of time. Many small business owners try to do Call to Action with an image-building budget. They don't have enough money to buy enough commercials across a wide range of media. Consequently, they won't achieve the levels of **reach** and **frequency** required for a successful sale or promotion.

Another pitfall of "BADvertising" is trying to implement a "media mix" on a small budget. The small business owner ends up spending small amounts of money with lots of different media. Because the budget is spread so thin, none of the media involved have sufficient budget to reach any meaningful levels of reach and frequency.

The proper way to implement a media mix is to build a schedule on **one medium that reaches a level of effective reach and frequency** before moving on to the next media choice.

A Word of Caution

It's easy for a business owner to mistakenly assume that good advertising is **all about the frequency** of the message, that is, flooding the market with their message will assure success. However, without a compelling creative message that speaks to the heart of the consumer, a business risks advertising their business into the "Zone of Irritation."

"An idea can turn to dust or magic depending on the talent that rubs against it."—William Bernbach, advertising pioneer and cofounder of Doyle Dane Bernbach advertising agency (1911-1982)

9

Compelling Creative Message—The Fourth Key

The Fourth Key to Advertising Success is having a Compelling Creative Message. Your advertising must differentiate you in the market, clearly articulating the unique value of your product or service. For the message to resonate with your prospective customer, it must evoke emotion or feeling. Engagement is the route to all successful advertising, and engagement is driven by emotion.

Engaging messages need an "easy on-ramp," that is, accessible, quick and immediate for the listener. Consumers will allow approximately 3 seconds for any one detail or part of the script to register an emotional response that they can relate to; otherwise, they will tune out the commercial.

Two approaches to the 3-second rule

It's important, then, to always keep in mind the 3-second rule making sure that everything in the script can be absorbed, reflected and responded to quickly. It is vital to keep the message as simple as possible with a single core idea to bring the commercial to life and make things happen around it. There are two ways to address this:

- The commercial itself is overridingly simple, giving the consumer easy onboard access. At the same time, there are novel ideas in the script and execution.

- There's some degree of complexity, but the ingredients that are familiar enough so that, once again, people have an easy onramp.

Four Creative Elements Every Ad Must Have

To be effective, every advertisement should include these four creative elements:

1. **The single most important word to the consumer:** *You.* The most important word **isn't** *sale* or *discount* or even *free*. The most important word to the consumer is the word **you**.
2. **The *felt need* of the consumer.** The felt need is something that the consumer feels: **emotion**. They think about it whenever the subject comes up. It is something that they want or need but haven't yet acted upon.

A good advertisement combines the first two creative elements early. For example:

> *"You love your home. But you hate your bathroom. It's small, it's cold and it's old-fashioned. You want a new bathroom."*

This first part of the advertisement has the most important word, ***you*** in it three times. And many of us can **identify with the felt need for a larger, warmer, more modern bathroom.**

3. **The *Call to Action*.** This important element describes what the consumer needs to do to address their felt need.

> *"Call the bathroom remodeling experts, ABC Bathrooms. They can make your bathroom dreams come true right before your very eyes."*

4. **Return On Investment**. This element tells the consumer what they'll get when they call or, more importantly, how their life will be better after calling ABC Bathrooms.

> *"Before you know it, you will be relaxing in your larger, warmer, more modern bathroom."*

Let the Professionals Handle It

Finally, a well-produced advertisement will use sound effects, an announcer and actors that will add polish and professionalism. All too often, a small business owner will want to play a role in the writing and producing of the advertisement. But it's important to realize that good advertisements are written from the perspective of the consumer, not the small business owner. The consumers see the business from the **outside in**, with "what's in it for me" at the forefront of their thoughts. In contrast, the small business owners tend to see the business from the **inside looking out** and focus on the features the business offers. For a feature to have any meaning to the consumer, the advertisement must **translate that feature into a benefit for the consumer**.

Marketing slogans like "we're family owned," "we're local," and "we have good prices" don't do much to motivate the savvy consumer in this competitive age. None of those features articulate any benefits for the consumer.

Instead, slogans like "the next time you have a backed up drain, call ABC Plumbing where there is never an extra charge for service on nights or weekends" will have better results. This slogan differentiates you from the competition with the feature that you do not charge extra for nights or weekends. If you're like me, it seems like it's always at night or on a weekend when I have a plumbing problem. Some might ask how ABC can afford not to charge extra on nights and weekends. With that kind of a positioning statement, ABC could charge a little bit more *all* the time.

Once a compelling creative message is crafted to your liking, put it on the air and just let it run and run. **Be patient and don't forget the First Key: *consistency***! Frequent changes in your message can sharply reduce campaign effectiveness. About the time *you* are tired of hearing your message is when consumers are just starting to take notice. The remaining chapters of this guide, which explain some fundamentals of consumer behavior and how customers make buying decisions, explain this in more detail.

If you find yourself becoming **impatient and tempted to ignore the Four Keys, please read and re-read these later chapters!** It takes time for customers to get to know you and to make decisions about your product or service. You'll realize that for advertising to work for your business, you will need apply all Four Keys to Advertising Success, including ***consistency***.

"The philosophy behind much advertising is based on the old observation that every man is really two men—the man he is and the man he wants to be."—William Feather, publisher (1889-1981)

10

The Psychology of Consumer Behavior

To use the Four Keys to Advertising Success effectively—that is, be more effective in your advertising and marketing efforts—you must know some basic principles about the psychology of consumer behavior.

Consumer behavior is driven by needs. **Maslow's Hierarchy of Needs** can be used as a basis for understanding why a consumer makes a decision to buy a product or a service.

In his 1943 paper *A Theory of Human Motivation*, Abraham Maslow proposed that the motivation for action is an unfulfilled need. Maslow's research suggests that humans seek to satisfy their needs and desires in a certain hierarchy. Maslow contends that people must satisfy their most basic needs first before they can go forward and satisfy the more sophisticated needs.

Physiological Needs: the Most Basic of Needs

The first level of basic needs is physiological. A human's physiological needs take the highest priority. The need to breathe is more important than anything else for your survival. Next, you need water. Water is more important than food because you can live longer without food than you can live without water. You need to have healthy bodily functions.

If these basic physiological needs are not met, an individual will de-prioritize all other activities until these basic needs are fulfilled. If these needs are not met, then the body will begin to deteriorate until the individual becomes ill and eventually dies.

Now, if you're wondering how Maslow's Hierarchy of Needs has anything to do with advertising, just consider how much Americans spend each year, and how much companies spend, on products and advertising addressing an individual's physiological needs of breathing, water, and bodily functions like sleeping and digestion:

- The top 14 pharmaceutical companies spent over $13 billion on advertising in 2008 for products like Spiriva, Advair and Symbicort.
- Americans spend over $15 billion dollars each year on bottled water. Aquafina (Pepsi) and Dasani (Coke) sell 24 percent of all U.S. bottled water. Yet, both are merely treated municipal tap water, resold to the public at a premium mark-up.
- U.S. consumers spend more than $3.6 billion a year on prescription sleep medications not to mention the amount of money spent on over-the-counter medications, homeopathic formulas, pillows, beds, mood music and even air sprays to help one sleep. The top three manufacturers of prescription sleep aids—Ambien, Lunesta and Rozerem—spent nearly three quarters of a billion dollars in pursuit of this market in 2006.
- Dannon spent $209 million in 2009 marketing dollars to position Activia yogurt as a brand that can help regulate digestion if eaten every day. Activia sold over $505 million in supermarket sales that year. Over $8 billion is spent annually on drugs to relieve indigestion and constipation, with additional billions spent annually advertising those drugs.

Safety: Another Basic Need

Safety is the next level of needs in Maslow's Hierarchy of Needs. People need to feel secure in their life. They are concerned for the safety and security of their families, their property and their future.

Broadview Security, formerly known as Brinks Security exploits this basic need for safety as the cornerstone of its marketing messages. In recent years, advertising for Broadview Security mostly features single women or women with small children in their homes when suddenly they are threatened by an intruder. But fortunately, an alarm goes off and the intruder flees because they are protected by a Broadview Security system.

Broadview has increased their advertising by more than 50 percent and annual sales have increased to more than a half a billion dollars.

Allstate Insurance recently introduced a marketing campaign *Protect Yourself from Mayhem*. The marketing message describes a number of worst-case scenarios where a consumer is exposed to risk; for example, a storm causes a tree to fall on a car and a distracted teen texting causes an accident. The Allstate website warns if you were to cause an accident, 9 percent of all cars on the road are luxury vehicles so you could be liable for the damage to a car costing $56,000 or more. The marketing message is "Mayhem is *everywhere;* nobody protects you better than Allstate."

One of the safety needs Maslow identified is the need for financial security, the security of revenues and resources. Banks and investment companies advertise to consumers with the knowledge of this basic human need. A common message illustrates the challenges and complexity of investing. Marketing messages routinely feature scenarios of doubt and anxiety for an individual's financial future. The messages pose questions about whether you are making the right decision or have enough saved up for retirement.

The chief marketing officer of Fidelity Investments used focus groups and customer insights to craft a marketing message to communicate that Fidelity Investments has the ability to help investors "navigate *all* stages of life." They concluded from their research that the majority of investor questions are derived directly from the life-stage events they are experiencing.

Moving to the Next Level: Social Needs

When an individual's physiological and safety needs are fulfilled, they can move up to the third level of needs in Maslow's model, the social needs. In contrast, when an individual doesn't feel their social needs are being met, their emotional and physical well-being begins to suffer. Loneliness can lead to social anxiety and depression. This often leads to serious physical illness and possibly even heart disease. The individual can often regress to the lower-level, more basic needs when they don't feel emotionally fulfilled.

Human beings have a natural need to be involved in emotionally based relationships. Whether those relationships come from large or small social groups, or one-on-one relationships, people need to love and be loved by others.

Advances in technology today allow people to satisfy this need to connect with others through social media like Facebook. More than half a billion people are now on Facebook sharing their personal information, their pictures and their stories with their Facebook *friends*. The phenomenal growth in users and advertising revenue at Facebook is fueled by this basic human need for social interaction identified by Maslow.

Not only is the membership growth at Facebook remarkable, advertising revenue at Facebook is growing exponentially from $700 million in 2009 to an estimated $2.14 billion in 2011. Facebook now generates more display advertising revenue than industry giant Yahoo.

You won't have to wait long to be exposed to advertising for one of the many dating sites promising the perfect relationship. They spend hundreds of millions of dollars on advertising.

On-line dating is big business. In 2010 Match Dot Com had over $400 million in revenue. Match Dot Com historically spends about half its revenue on advertising to bring new users in the door (and through the subscription pay wall). They added 5.4 million paying members in 2009 and 6.9 million of them in 2010.

Social media and on-line dating are not the only ones that advertise to the consumer's need to be involved socially with others. It's a very common tactic used by many product categories.

The largest casual dining chain in America, Applebee's International, has long tried to position itself as a local gathering place with the theme of "Eatin' good in the neighborhood." Their commercials feature happy people getting together with friends and family for more than just a good meal. The advertising slogan at Olive Garden is "When you're here, you're Family" is another example. Even Lowe's Home Improvement Centers are getting in on the action with their slogan, "Let's build something together."

The Need for Esteem

The next level in Maslow's Hierarchy of Needs is the need for esteem. According to Maslow's studies, people want and need to be respected. We also have a need to feel good about ourselves; we need our own self-respect. We need people we can look up to in life. Respecting role models and leaders is something Maslow identified as part of our need for esteem.

The National Car Rental advertising campaign script appeals to the need for esteem with the following script: "You are a business pro, executor of efficiency; you can spot an amateur from a mile away, and you rent from National." Another example is the most memorable of all McDonalds advertising campaigns: *You deserve a break today.*

At the Top: Self Actualization

At the pinnacle of Maslow's Hierarchy of Needs is the need for self-actualization, the instinctual need of humans to make the most of their unique abilities and to strive to be the best they can be. In short, self-actualization is reaching one's fullest potential.

The United States Army created a very compelling message using the appeal to this instinctual need for self-actualization with the *Be All That You Can Be, In the Army* campaign.

Advertising for higher education, degree completion programs and technical colleges appeal to the instinctual need for self-actualization. Commercials for ITT Technical Institute describe the dangers of identity theft and corporate computer crimes to articulate the need to qualified individuals to learn the latest computer technology for the jobs in this field.

Needs and Emotions: the Core of Consumer Behavior

When you understand the psychology of consumer behavior, you begin to understand that you are not just selling a product, you are selling the **idea** of the product, the **image** of the product, and the **result** of the product. We are essentially promising to fulfill one or more of the needs in the hierarchy.

At the core of any purchase is an **emotional** reason that is driving the consumer behavior. There is an old sales adage that goes like this: "Home Depot sells millions of drill bits every year, not because people want a drill bit but because people have a need to drill a hole. But people don't really want a hole in their wall do they? They need a hole in the wall to mount a hook that will hold that beautiful new family portrait."

Human behavior is influenced by many things, but the most influential key to advertising success are the **needs** and the **emotions** the consumer experiences that are related to your products. Advertising and branding are most effective when the message can establish an emotional connection with the audience that tells a story of why your business is the right one for their needs and desires.

The next chapters delve into consumer awareness and the consumer's decision-making process. You will learn that people don't just rush out and buy something when they hear or see and advertisement. **They go through a process that usually takes longer than you would like.** If you're in a hurry to sell your products or services, **having a sale or a special promotion usually doesn't speed up the process**. All you do is give away your hard-earned profit margin to someone who was probably already going to buy from you. The next two chapters on consumer awareness and decision-making will help you avoid these and other costly mistakes and, instead, practice **all** *Four Keys to Advertising Success*—especially ***consistency***.

"The man who stops advertising to save money is like the man who stops the clock to save time."—Thomas Jefferson, American President (1743-1826)

11

Advertising Creates Awareness

Small business owners are often surprised when they learn that advertising alone doesn't make people buy things. It doesn't cause people to come into your store or call you on the phone.

Those are the intended consequences of good advertising. Advertising can do only one thing for your business: create **awareness** about your business. Advertising can let people know who you are, where you are and what you can do for them. People enter the market to buy a product or a service **when they have a need or a desire**, not because they are exposed to advertising.

Awareness Is Mind Share

This awareness of your business within the marketplace is called mind share. **Mind share is the percentage of the population that recalls your business name** when asked to name a business within your product category.

Mind share, or the development of consumer awareness or popularity, is one of the main objectives of advertising and promotion. When people think of examples of a product type or category, they usually think of a limited number of brand names. For example, a prospective buyer of a college education will have several thousand colleges to choose from. However, the evoked set, or set of schools considered, will probably be limited to about 10. Of these 10, the colleges most familiar with the buyer will receive the greatest attention.

Mind Share Is Market Share

Actually, mind share can be measured. When a small business owner advertises, over time, the mind share increases. Likewise, when a small business owner stops advertising or cuts back, the number of people in the market that recalls that business name first, begins to decline.

Mind share equals market share. Targeted customers need to **know** you before they **need** you. People buy things when they have a need or a desire. Eighty six percent of respondents say they are "likely or very likely" to shop with the first name they think of when the need or desire surfaces.

However, the same research discovered that across many popular product categories, the number of consumers who couldn't think of a name was remarkably high. In some cases as many as 80 percent of the respondents couldn't think of the name of a business when prompted with a random business category.

This is fantastic news for a company looking to grow their market share. There are many consumers out there without a clear-cut preference in a wide range of common business categories. This is the upside potential for a company that embarks on a consistent branding campaign.

The vast majority of purchases are consumer-driven, meaning, the need or desire comes from within them. Advertising to build mind share ensures that when those needs and desires bubble up for products or services you offer, the consumer thinks about your business first.

Marketers try to maximize the popularity of their product, so that the brand coexists with deeper, more empirical categories of objects. Kleenex, for example, can distinguish itself as a type of tissue. But, because it has gained popularity among consumers, it is frequently used as a term to identify any tissue, even if it is from a competing brand. Similarly, the term "googling," describing the act of on-line searching, was derived from the Internet search engine Google.

A legal risk of such popularity is that the name may become so widely accepted that it becomes a generic term and loses trademark protection. Examples include "escalator," "chapstick," "tupperware" and "bandaid."

Although these are extreme examples of **mind share**, the **premise** remains the same for businesses large and small: **to increase short or long term sales, market share, product information and reputation, you must first focus on building your mind share**.

"In any moment of decision, the best thing you can do is the right thing, the next best thing is the wrong thing, and the worst thing you can do is nothing."—Theodore Roosevelt, American President (1858-1919)

12

The Decision Journey

The customer's "decision journey" can be short or long, depending on the type of product or service. For example, a car purchase usually involves a long decision journey, while grocery shopping involves a short decision journey. Whether quick or well thought out, virtually every buying decision is driven by some kind of event that triggers the need or a desire for a particular product or service.

When the consumer begins the process of selecting a product or service to satisfy a **"triggering event,"** they have a pool of options to choose from. During this evaluation phase of the decision journey, the consumer will **add and subtract different brands** as they learn more about their choices. As the consumer learns more, their selection criteria can change too. This is more a function of the consumer's search for more information rather than advertising and marketing.

The Triggering Event: the First Stop on the Decision Journey

The decision journey begins when a consumer has a **triggering event.** A triggering event is something that happens in the consumer's life; it happens on the consumer's timetable and no amount of advertising can change that. It is the triggering event that changes the status quo for the consumer. It is the triggering event that triggers the need or the desire for a product or a service.

When a consumer has a triggering event, they begin to evaluate brands that are top-of-mind, the brands that the consumer thinks of first. They think of these brands first because they have been exposed to advertising, in-store displays or an encounter with the product through a friend or acquaintance.

For example, a plumber could advertise all day long, discount here, discount there, savings this, savings that. Most people won't call regardless of the offer because they don't have a leaking pipe or a plumbing project on the horizon. They simply don't have the need or the desire no matter how much the plumber advertises or discounts the price.

Another example could be a body shop that repairs cars after a collision. It doesn't matter how much the body shop advertises or what kind of a discount or special they offer, if the consumer doesn't have any damage to their car, they simply won't respond.

Did the advertising work? Yes, it did. People saw or heard the message, they simply said "no" to the offer because they didn't have the need or desire.

This is a good example why, in most cases, offering a discount or a special price does nothing to further your efforts to establish yourself on the Ladder of Importance (more about that later). The plumber who advertises a special price may be seen or heard by the consumer, but because there is no need or desire, the consumer says no to the offer. And since the offer is time-sensitive and discount-based, the brain quickly forgets the message and moves on to other tasks.

The plumber and the body shop are examples of immediate triggering events in product categories that are not frequently used. Other **triggering events take more time to develop.**

The mother of all triggering events is a couple getting married. Not only does the couple spend money but so do the parents, brothers, sisters, grandparents, aunts, uncles, cousins and friends on both sides of the family. This new couple needs everything to start a household.

Starting a family is a triggering event. It triggers the need for medical services, perhaps a new home or a remodeling project, baby clothes, baby furniture, car seat, insurance, day care, toys and the list goes on and on.

A kid growing up is a triggering event to buy new clothes that fit. A change in season may trigger the need for warmer clothes. Getting tired of the lime green paint in the kitchen is a triggering event to repaint with a new color. Renewal time is a triggering event for insurance, especially if the premiums go up.

Virtually every purchase decision is preceded by some form of a triggering event. Without the triggering event, there is little need or desire for the product, regardless of the offer. With the exception of businesses that experience high-frequency purchasing, like food, fuel and other consumables, **having a sale is not a triggering event**. It is very likely that offering a discount only gives away your hard-earned profit margin to someone who was probably going to shop with you anyway.

Roadblocks on the Journey

We live in the over-communicated society. The average consumer is exposed to over 5,000 commercial messages every single day. With the proliferation of new technology, the flow of information will only increase. Studies on the human brain have determined that it can process only so much information before reaching "sensory overload." At some point, the brain simply can't keep up with the flow of information and just stops processing. Much like a sponge can only hold so much water, the brain can only process so much information. There are some **physical** roadblocks in the brain that prevent most advertising from leaving a lasting impression.

The human brain has some built-in features that help it manage the massive amounts of information we are exposed to every day. These are the roadblocks to your advertising. The reticular cortex is the part of the brain that controls awareness or alertness. It is the reticular cortex that is constantly scanning our surroundings for the important information we need for survival. All sensory information flows through the reticular cortex first on the way to other parts of the brain for processing. The reticular cortex acts as the dispatch system in the brain and **determines the priority** of sensory data and routes that data on for further processing **or discards the information** as nonessential and sets it aside.

The reticular cortex checks all sensory data against our "mental database of needs and desires" and if there is no match for this new information, it is simply disregarded and quickly forgotten. Professor Hermann Ebbinghaus was a German psychologist who pioneered the experimental study of memory. Ebbinghaus was the first person to describe the learning curve.

But Ebbinghaus also discovered the **forgetting curve**. The forgetting curve describes the exponential curve that illustrates how fast we tend to forget new information. The sharpest decline is in the first 20 minutes, then in the first hour, and then the curve evens off after about one day.

Ebbinghaus' research was done over 120 years ago, long before the information age, long before the onslaught of mass media and information technology. It is hard to imagine that the information overload of today doesn't speed up the forgetting curve in the mind of the present-day consumer.

Unfortunately, for many local business owners trying to advertise their business, the brain rejects much of what it sees and hears on a daily basis. The brain tends to accept information that fits into previously established perceptions and is **relevant to the individual's needs and desires**.

The Ladder of Importance

Once "accepted" information enters our brain, we tend to organize our thoughts in order of preference, putting the things we like most at the top of our list. List-building is a key organizational characteristic of the human brain because of the vast amount of information we are exposed to and our own natural limitations.

In their book, *Positioning, the battle for your mind,* Jack Trout and Al Ries first introduced the metaphor of a mental ladder to help explain how the brain classifies information. The product or service you like the most within a given product category will be on the top rung of the ladder. Your second preference will be on the second rung, your third preference on rung number three and so on. Imagine a different ladder in your mind for each different product category.

When a consumer places your business name on their ladder, they have placed your name into their memory. But how many rungs can there be on a ladder? How many names can people remember?

Harvard psychologist Dr. George A. Miller is the author of *The Magical Number Seven, Plus or Minus Two*. In this highly respected work, Miller presents his findings on the study of memory performance. Miller observed that working memory has limitations; we can keep track of only so many things at one time. His work suggests that our memory span is around seven elements at a time, but the limits of memory span vary by the type of information. Subjects recall numbers (seven items) better than letters (six) and letters better than words (five). Memory span is also influenced by the length of time, and how familiar we are, with the elements.

With so many factors influencing working memory, Miller proposed that the memory span in young adults was four to seven items, less with children and older adults. Nonetheless, as Jack Trout and Al Ries suggest, each product category has a different ladder. But some ladders will be longer than others depending on the importance of, and your interest level in, that category.

The value of a position on the Ladder of Importance is significant. History suggests that the company that **ranks at the top very often has** twice as much market share as the company on the next rung and that company has twice as much market share as the company on the third rung. If your company isn't in the top few positions, there isn't much market share left over.

The **goal of any advertising plan should be to rank in the top position** on the Ladder of Importance within your product category. However, merely flooding the market with your message won't elevate your business to the top rung of the Ladder of Importance. Without an **emotional** message that speaks to the heart of the consumer, your business risks advertising into the "Zone of Irritation." Remember, it takes **all** four of the *Four Keys to Advertising Success* to reach the top of the Ladder. You must have a **consistent** plan that has the proper balance of both **reach** and **frequency** for your budget and your **message must be relevant to the consumer's needs and desires.**

The Buyer's Awareness Cycle: the Middle of the Decision Journey

The period of time between the actual triggering event and the eventual purchase is called the Buyer's Awareness Cycle. The consumer passes through **four distinct phases of cognitive thought** as they move from being 1) just an **ordinary person** with no need or desire for the product, then they become 2) a **prospect**, then they become 3) a **researcher** and then eventually 4) a **buyer**.

The length of time a consumer spends in the Buyer's Awareness Cycle will vary from a few days, weeks, months and even years, depending on the product category and the amount of money required. It is during the Buyer's Awareness Cycle that real preferences are formed. But it's hard to recognize the process is underway because people in the Buyer's Awareness Cycle are not walking around with a large sign advertising that they are a potential customer. These **prospects** and **researchers** are largely *invisible* to the business owner but they are *seriously* in the market.

The Dangers of Discounting

When a local business owner sets out to learn about advertising, they often imitate or mimic what they perceive to be successful advertising. They often try to do **Call to Action advertising**. That's when you see or hear an advertisement for a product or service with a big discount. The advertisement says that the offer is only available for a short period of time so you "must act now," "you must call before midnight tonight," "sale ends Saturday." Make no mistake about it, Call to Action advertising can be very successful if you have enough money to do it properly. It can literally take thousands of dollars a day to do effective Call to Action advertising.

Unfortunately, most advertising you see and hear today is driven by the desire for **instant gratification.** Consequently, many business owners **focus their marketing** efforts on the **buyers** and not the prospects or the researchers. Their advertising messages are largely focused on those consumers in the final stage of the Buyer's Awareness Cycle, when the prospect is ready to make a purchase. The business advertises price and item information in an attempt to get the buyer to shop with them. This strategy ignores the very important **research** phases the consumer goes through in the Buyer's Awareness Cycle when real preferences and buying decisions are formed, **based on value**, not on a low price or a special offer.

Business owners believe that a discount price or a special offer moves a prospect into the market for what they have to offer, when all it really does is give away their hard-earned profit margin to someone who already was likely to shop with them anyway. Price and item advertising gives a business owner a false sense of their ability to track their advertising effectiveness because the customers will either mention they heard or saw the ad, or they will bring the ad in when they come to shop.

Too many marketing plans advertise **only to the buyers** and not the prospects and researchers. Little thought is given to attracting the prospects and researchers while they are in the Buyer's Awareness Cycle. This is unfortunate because it is *not* the most useful strategy for long-term business success. The consumers start to think of the business as a discounter and will come to expect nothing more than just a low price. This **erodes the hard-earned profit margins** and puts the future of the business at risk as it tries to compete on **price** and not on **value**.

Consumers move into the market for a particular product or a service **because of the triggering event, not because of the discount price**. Once the consumer recognizes this need or desire, they enter the Buyer's Awareness Cycle and begin their search for the product or service that will satisfy their triggering event. By the time a consumer reaches the buying phase of the Buyer's Awareness Cycle, **two-thirds have already formed an opinion** on how to satisfy their triggering event **before price ever becomes an issue**.

Successful marketing and advertising recognizes that the buying process originates with the **triggering event**. The consumer moves from being a **prospect** to a **researcher before** they become a **buyer**. Two-thirds of the decision-making process is accomplished during the research phases of the Buyer's Awareness Cycle, only about one-third arrive at the buying phase without a clear preference. Strategies that focus simply on the buyers are missing the real opportunity to influence the decision-making process. Getting your message out on a **consistent** basis during all phases of the Buyer's Awareness Cycle helps the **researchers** include you in the purchase decision.

The AIDA (awareness/interest/desire/action) Funnel

E. St. Elmo Lewis (1872-1948) was an American businessman who spent his life promoting and teaching other businesspeople about the benefits of advertising. Lewis was a cofounder of the Association of National Advertisers in 1910. Today, the ANA's membership now includes over 400 companies with 9,000 brands. These companies collectively spend over $100 billion a year in advertising and marketing. It is the Association of National Advertisers who is responsible for many of the standards that drive the advertising industry today.

Back in 1898, Lewis was trying to explain the effects of advertising and the influence advertising has in the buying process. Lewis determined that consumers pass through four cognitive faces in their decision making process. He described the process as the AIDA Funnel.

The AIDA Funnel can help describe what consumers experience when they find themselves in the Buyer's Awareness Cycle after a triggering event. As a funnel, the model illustrates that not every consumer who has a triggering event ends up making a purchase. This is helpful to know when setting expectations.

The first cognitive phase of thought is the **Awareness Stage**. If you have a car wreck, you are immediately **aware that you have a need** for repairs. If there is water in the basement, you are very immediately that you need a plumber.

But within many product categories, the process of becoming aware of a need or desire can be more gradual and take more time. Waking up one morning and finally deciding you can't take that lumpy old mattress is definitely awareness that you want a new mattress.

Once a consumer is aware or their need or desire, they must move through the second phase, the **Interest Stage**. This is the logical stage of the process where the consumer is **analytical, rational and objective**. They may start to ask around to members of their family or their friends for advice. They might go on the Internet and do some research. The consumer must work up the interest to do something about the need or desire.

If someone has an accident in their old pickup truck and it was their fault and they don't have enough money to fix it, they may not make it past the Interest Stage of the AIDA Funnel.

For whatever reason, it's going to take too much time, it's going to cost too much money or they don't know where to go, a lot of triggering events don't result in a sale.

When you are advertising your business, your message about how your company can reduce the time required, how you company can make it affordable and how your company is the one the consumer can trust, is essential in moving the prospect past the Interest Stage.

Once a consumer has made it through the Interest Stage, the **Desire Stage** takes over. This is when the consumer really works up their **desire to spend the money**. They've done all of the logical research and everything seems in order. Now the **emotions** start to come out. The consumer really wants to get the product or service. Both the **Interest** and the **Desire** Stages work hand-in-hand at this point.

Once the consumer has worked their way through the Awareness, Interest and Desire Stages, they are ready to take Action. They are ready to spend. The **Action Stage is very short**, usually 24-48 hours. It is short because the consumer has done almost all of the work necessary to be **ready to spend**. Because the Action Stage is so short and the prospect is ready to buy, a business owner will often mistake this eagerness as a result of a sale price and not the result of the time spent in the decision journey. In other words, this eagerness to buy sends a false signal to the business owner that can cause you to stray from the first key to advertising success, ***consistency***.

The Changing Shapes of the Decision Journey

Marketing scholars now believe that instead of a funnel-shaped process, a decision journey can look more like a bowling pin. Rather than systematically narrowing their choices, the consumer is likely to add and subtract brands from a group under consideration during an **extended** evaluation phase. A good example would be prospective car buyers who begin their research a year or more before they plan to replace their current vehicles.

When the consumer begins the process of selecting a product or service to satisfy a triggering event, they have a pool of options to choose from. But as they explore those options, it is now clear that the pool of options expands instead of grows smaller, especially with the search power of the Internet. As the consumer researches their choices, the process pulls in information and opinions from various sources: advertising, research and other people.

For many product categories, the first stop on the Internet is not Google, Yahoo or Bing, it is Amazon Dot Com or Consumer Reports Dot Com. Consumers want to know how other people feel about the product or service they need or desire.

The opinions of other people is called **consumer advocacy** and it is very influential in the decision journey. Consumer advocacy has been around forever. A couple of friends are having a cup of coffee, one complains about their transmission acting up on their car. The other friend suggests a local repair shop that took great care of them when they had a problem.

Consumer advocacy is very powerful; it can often override price concerns because the opinion is coming from an existing customer or someone the prospect trusts.

Consumer advocacy goes back to a very important point: Your *brand* is what your customers say about you when they are describing their consumer experience with your business.

The bowling pin model also applies to short decision journeys, especially in today's fast-paced society with constant information. The proliferation of mobile devices is causing a seismic shift in consumer behavior. When you get hungry, for example, you may spend all of 15 minutes in that decision journey. You can actually conduct product research while you are standing in the aisle of the store. Smart phones can scan a bar code and link to a web page with information. The consumer can even watch a short video about the product. But this only reinforces the need to **be known before you are needed.**

Regardless of the diagram depicting a decision journey, remember that **good advertising builds mind share**. Good advertising communicates a positive message about your business and how you can satisfy needs and desires. Eighty six percent of the consumers surveyed said they were "likely or very likely" to shop with the **first name they think of** when they have the triggering event.

Don't let your potential customers get lost along their decision journey and end up at your competition. Make the commitment to be **consistent** with your advertising; it is the First Key to Advertising Success.

"As long as the earth endures, seedtime and harvest, cold and heat, summer and winter, day and night will never cease."—Genesis 8:22

13

Parting Thoughts: The Law of Seed Time to Harvest

There are natural laws that govern our world. Just like in life, the Law of Seed Time to Harvest applies to the consumer psychology and behavior affecting your company. You can't work against the principle of Seed Time to Harvest. It impacts everything and everybody. We are all affected by the Law of Seed Time to Harvest. Now, while many things change in this world, the Law of Seed Time to Harvest never changes.

Farmers know that they must plow their fields, plant their seeds, water and fertilize their crops and then harvest them in due time. An Iowa corn farmer would love to plant a corn crop in April and reap a harvest a few weeks later in May but it just doesn't work that way. The soil temperature and moisture need to be just right for the seed to germinate. The proper mix of nutrients must be present for the seed to grow. The farmer must fight off weeds and insects. It all takes time. But when the harvest comes in, the results are worth the wait.

In the world of marketing, you plant the seeds with your advertising messages of what you can do for the customer when they have a need or a desire for what you have to offer. You water and fertilize that seed in the consumer's mind with a consistent ongoing message. You harvest that seed as a new customer when that customer has a need or a desire.

In business, the Law of Seed Time to Harvest is driven by the consumer buying cycle. Consumers have a tendency to buy things in cycles. For example, if you buy a new car, you'll be out of the market for another car until you come around in the cycle a few years from now. Once you buy that new car, other car dealers can no longer harvest you as a new customer. You're out of the market until the cycle is repeated and you're in the market for a car again. It doesn't matter how much advertising you are exposed to, you're out of the market for the next few years.

When you plant your seeds of advertising with a consistent plan, your seeds will grow deep roots into the consumer's mind. Deep roots anchor your advertising message so that it is not easily swept away by the winds of the competition's inconsistent advertising message.

The Law of Seed Time to Harvest is in your hands. You control the type of seed you plant. Understanding the principles of Seed Time to Harvest can change your life. If you want a good crop you must sow your best seed. You cannot sow "nothing" and expect to reap "something."

Be Patient . . . . Success Will Happen

Over the years, I've presented *The Four Keys to Advertising Success* to over 30,000 business owners across 26 states. The business owners who use the Four Keys—while remembering basic business fundamentals and the psychological fundamentals about consumer behavior, and resisting the temptation for instant gratification—*consistently* report that after four to six months they start to feel more satisfied with their advertising efforts.

Made in the USA
San Bernardino, CA
03 October 2013